My German Dictionary

Katherine Hollander

WAYWISER

First published in 2019 by

THE WAYWISER PRESS

Christmas Cottage, Church Enstone, Chipping Norton, Oxfordshire, OX7 4NN, UK
P.O. Box 6205, Baltimore, MD 21206, USA
https://waywiser-press.com

Editor-in-Chief
Philip Hoy

Senior American Editor
Joseph Harrison

Associate Editors
Eric McHenry | Dora Malech | V. Penelope Pelizzon | Clive Watkins
Greg Williamson | Matthew Yorke

A CIP catalogue record for this book is available from the British Library

ISBN: 978-1-904130-97-0

Printed and bound by
T. J. International Ltd., Padstow, Cornwall, PL28 8RW

My German Dictionary

for John
and
for my mother

Acknowledgments

I am grateful to the literary magazines in which some of these poems previously appeared, sometimes in slightly different form. "General Strike, 1920," was published in *236*, "Great War" in *Pleiades*, and "The Wounded Soldier" in *Slate*. "War Suite" and "Niemand" were published in *Sugar House Review*. "Ikon for Osip Mandelstam" was published on a limited-edition broadside by Scott Sell in November 2008. "Ikon for Rosa Luxemburg," "Ikon for Käthe Kollwitz," and "Ikon for Karl Kautsky" appeared in *The Common Online*. The whole of the *Book of Ikons* was produced as a large-format book with monoprint illustrations, in a limited edition of two copies, in May 2011, in collaboration with the artist Alla Lazebnik. "Brecht in Hollywood," "Die Courage" and "Die Hexe" were published in *Spork*. "Der Anfang" was published in *Literary Imagination*. "Der Bär" was published in *Tupelo Quarterly* and was a finalist for the journal's inaugural poetry contest. "Die Pferde" and "Die Seele" were published as "Horses (Franz Marc)" and "Die Seele (The Soul)"in *Hunger Mountain*. "Der Tod" was published in *Root Quarterly*.

My thanks to the Vermont Studio Center and the Brechts Hus, Svendborg, Denmark.

"The Wounded Soldier" owes a debt to Nathan Hoks. "Das Lebenwohl" borrows two lines adapted with permission from Jessica Yuan, with gratitude.

"Dunkel" is a radical re-imagining of Bertolt Brecht's poem "An die Nachgeborenen" as if spoken by his wife, the actress Helene Weigel. In "Ikon for Karl Kaustky," the remark about "the last two men of German social democracy" refers to Rosa Luxemburg and Clara Zetkin, and is actually attributed not to Kautsky but to August Bebel. In "Sophie and Escha, 1929," the dichotomy of "red assimilationist" and "Jewish fascist" comes from Hannah Arendt's essay on Walter Benjamin; the associational groups to which the sisters belong are invented, if similar to those which really existed.

Acknowledgments

"Sophie and Escha, 1929" is for Carrie Cleveland. "The Wounded Soldier" is for my father and stepmother. "War Suite" is for my

brother, Sam Hollander. "Die Familie" is for Silvia Beier and Peter Schwarz. "Ohne" is for Cory Elizabeth Nelson, who believes in this book. "Brecht in Svendborg" is for Sheila Gray Jordan because she asked to hear it twice. "Zusammen" is for John A. Coakley, always.

Four people intervened in the life of this book without whom it would not exist as a book: Sarah Green, Talia Neffson, Dora Malech, and Charles Wright. Thank you.

I want to express my gratitude to T. Hunter Wilson, Dana Howell, Timothy F. Little, Robert Pinsky, Louise Glück, Brina Caplan, Scott (Skip) Sell, Chloe Martinez, Brandy and Kevin Barents, Austyn Ellese Mayfield, Onna Solomon, Joshua Mehigan, Heidi Hart, Bekah and Jeff Stout, Amos Worth, Christina Kimball Ingersoll and her family, Caroline and the Loomis Gang, Jim Schmidt, Jonathan Zatlin, Sarah L. Leonard, Michael Holm, Tanya Larkin, Sandra Lim, Adrian Blevins, Sarah Braunstein, Arisa White, Ryan Harper and Lynn Casteel Harper, Mary Ellis Gibson, Nano Taggart, Natalie Young, Elaine Johanson, and Wes McNair. Daniel Abrahams, Yang Fan, Jennifer Meredith, Jerzy Wieczorek, and Lauren Yoshizawa deserve special mention for rolling with my very quick and unexpected costume changes between historian and poet and finding ways to support both roles this past year. Thank you Helen Bresler, Tara Cates, Franklin Crump, and Jen Lenz, for feeding me. Thank you Henry. Thank you to my extended families: Marlboro, Coakley/Gantz, Hollander, and Gortych/Team Barbara. Love and gratitude especially to my father Michael Hollander, my stepmother Janna Hobbs, my brother Sam Hollander, and to Barbara Gortych, my unfailing and brilliant mother. My very sweetest thanks to my partner John A. Coakley.

In memoriam: Frank Reeve, Ruth Hollander, and the one and only Christopher, wise spirits.

Contents

Contents

Foreword by Charles Wright

                                    The good
         traveling coat has a fox-fur collar

         and a fat gold tassel at the shoulder.
         Pull on it, and from the wide sleeve a little
         cedar ladder nudges out, ready to take you away.

And does it ever! What an unexpected ending to the poem and beginning to the book. A book of startling, radiant images that ferry the poems to their destinations of discovery and illumination.

Such a journey can often be difficult or go in circles. That does not happen in this wonderful book. There is a cedar ladder, a kind of under-narrative whose images connect with each other in ways that keep the poems moving, and the reader climbing: the ladder pulls the reader on, and delivers the poem at the end, whole and dripping light.

I suspect that most, if not all of us, have signature poems that we love, and continue to love, all our lives. This generally happens when we are young and most susceptible to the marvel of new poems. I myself have several that have stunned me and altered my way of seeing things: "Blandula, Tenulla, Vagula," by Ezra Pound; "Afternoons," by Philip Larkin; "Because I Could Not Stop For Death," by Emily Dickinson—not the best work by all three, but wonderful poems. I also suspect that there are several poems in this book that very well may be the touchstones to young writers in the years to come. Poems from "The Alphabet," for instance, or perhaps from the first part of the book. All it takes is a couple of images, or a particular rhythm, and you're hooked.

I have been talking about images, and how they rise up so unexpectedly and delightfully. But there is a vocal vision as well that runs like a fine thread throughout this book. The tension of voice and the suspension of voice where the poems demand seem extraordinarily strong and insistent and give the language its vibrancy and sting. It gives it authority. It gives it a certain quality of grace.

Look, these are wise and brave poems, from a wise and brave hand, A to Z. They go to the heart of the heart of the matter, whatever it is, and wherever it is. Like sharp little picks, they de-ice and reveal. If less is more (as I believe it is), then this introduction is much more. I have tried to point out what I believe is the core power of these poems. I have tried to suggest the music that is inherent in their language. I have tried to say what a beautiful and—it seems to me—necessary book it is. And now I will withdraw behind the curtain as it sets out, like a gleaming gondola on the waters of literature, the tricky but welcoming waters of literature.

"Today, in a German dictionary, I saw *elend*
And the heart in my breast turned over, it was—"

Randall Jarrell, "Seele im Raum"

Confession (Invitation)

I couldn't be a good Jew, so I tried
to be a good historian. I couldn't be
a good historian, so I wrote poems.

I couldn't write about the Shoah, so
I wrote about the Somme. My heart
is not a pocket watch. I wrote swans

snails, stars, and mud. I couldn't sleep,
so I tried sleepwalking. I couldn't
sleepwalk, so I just dreamed. Oh

doctor-father, oak-owl, grandfather clock:
Why didn't you help godpapa? Why didn't you help
me? *Nuremburg, Nuremburg, my old hometown.*

Tell me, however should I find such a country?
I didn't love a nation, I loved an idea.
I don't trust policemen, I don't look

at stray dogs, I don't trust clocks. *I am
unpacking my library. Yes, I am.* The good
traveling coat has a fox-fur collar

and a fat gold tassel at the shoulder.
Pull on it, and from the wide sleeve a little
cedar ladder nudges out, ready to take you away.

I.

Answers to the Question Europe

I.

In a leaf-printed apron,
I was standing at the window.
I pressed the seams of the dumplings,
slipped them into the boiling pot.
Outside the kitchen, the sea
arranged itself in green pews.
Then a white bull emerged out of them,
and looked me straight in the eye.
I rode side-saddle on his damp back,
sowing the dumplings behind me
where they floated like little boats

not making a path I could follow home.

II.

My mother was a Polish Catholic.
My father was a Russian Jew. They
met at a university that soared
like a schooner atop a sea of wheat
and corn: lush yellow billows, the sky
a Prussian blue. Then the snow began
its never-ending overture. When I was born,
Freud was my babysitter. They say
I grew up with a Viennese accent, but

you shouldn't believe what you hear.

III.

When I was sixteen, I was sent away
to the south of France. We drove down
the coast, stopped for a meal outdoors:
an avalanche of tiny golden fish,
each crisp as a relic and salty as heaven,
heaped on my plate like church treasure.
The sun, it blinded you. I was lost
and happy. At noon, the cathedral door
opened and a priest led forth the newly baptized,
bawling in their mothers' arms, holy water

leaving their heads in clouds of steam.

IV.

I slept under a blanket of nations.
Germany was green, Russia pink
and gold. At the foot of the bed, a lady
was sewing. How the borders ached
where her needed pierced them!
After a while, I couldn't sleep. The patchwork
was coming apart, letting in the cold
from the wide-open window. Bears and lions,
no bigger than mice, snarled at one another
from the pockets of her gown. Tiny eagles and airplanes

circled the airspace over my head.

V.

I dreamed I found a black cat half-dead
in the back street. Its blood made continent-
shaped prints on my sleeves. It looked
as though it had been in a terrible fight, but I knew
it had savaged itself. Its ears were ripped
and bitten out in little islands. I took it in
and rubbed it with a towel. I put a dish
of fresh water before it. The fire warmed
its lush reddish coat. As I watched,
it fell asleep. As I watched, it woke.
It opened its eyes, and showed me
its beautiful paws, which it held out

pink as soap, like little cameos.

VI.

I met a man in a café. He was drinking
sable coffee from a cup and saucer. His eyes
were shy, almond-shaped, and sly, his curls
lined up on his brow like snails in twilight.
Where his shirt was open, his throat shone
like a star. His white bed tossed like a little boat
in a storm. He said, *I am every poet
slaughtered, every revolutionary starved.*
He kissed me on the forehead, said *Now
you are marked with my own seal, and every word
you write will be a letter home, every
analysis, even the most subtle, will fly*

to my heart like a white valentine, my sister.

Sophie and Escha, 1929

Two sisters from Silesia, working for the university as calculators
in the department of Astronomy & Physics, sitting all day in a
room full of other hardheaded young women adding enormous
columns of numbers, multiplying stars.

They look like silent film actresses—dark hair, dark eyes, sharp
dark lips and white faces. They both wear black dresses and white
dickeys. They each have a pair of maryjanes the color of black
cherries, with a mother-of-pearl button on the strap.

On Friday nights, Sophie pins on her red armband and takes the
minutes for the neighborhood Young Spartakists League. Escha
lights candles and sings sad songs with her friends from the
Zionist Youth Brigade.

On Saturday mornings they like to drink coffee and catch up on
their reading in their kimonos. Escha's kimono is decorated with
pears, Sophie's with chrysanthemums. They are both partial to the
feuilletons of Joseph Roth and the cartoons of Georg Grosz. Käthe
Kollwitz makes them cry. Escha reads *Der Jude*. Sophie reads *Das
Tagebuch*. They lost their brother in the Great War and his portrait
regards them tenderly from behind its bud vase. The Berlin
sunshine comes onto the table and lights up the crumbs.

On Sundays they have terrific arguments. No one who knows
them could imagine them screaming the way they do. They indict
one another's political affiliations. Their skin becomes blotchy.
Escha calls Sophie *a Red Assimilationist!* Sophie calls Escha *a
Jewish fascist!* The lily of the valley in the bud vase trembles on
its stalk like the passion of their delicate brother. When they are
finished, they cry a little, they do their hair, they put on their nice
dresses, they pin on their hats, they link arms in their cherry-
colored shoes and go out to take in, go out to the cinema or the
zoo, the theater of Weimar.

General Strike, Berlin 1920

From the dark apartment
the street is an unlit hallway.
The tall lamps hang their heads
like tired horses.

Inside, the unseen wallpaper
is soft against the walls.
The room swims in darkness.
A man, a woman, a girl.

At home all day, they have been shy
with one another, unused to idleness.
They have read the paper, talked
a little. Now the woman stands

at the stove, one burner on,
a blue water lily of light.
In the pot, the stew is rich
and black. The man sits at the table

his hands open like gray gloves.
The girl lifts a dish and light
licks its edge like a tongue of oil.
She passes the dish to her mother.

The woman fills it with the dark stew.
The man lifts his spoon like a beacon.

Great War

How they are wreathed
and anointed, they that went off
with deep knapsacks. That sleep now
in one another's arms in the damp trenches,
drugged with death. Who bled
their hearts' blood in bombed stables,
the horses spooked or quiet
in the smell of straw.

In old nurseries, where the nightlight
burns like a sleepless heart
the sisters and beloveds dream visitations
from boys with white lips, cold hands, cold
kisses that ripple through the body like coins in a pond.
Watch the dead youths holding one another
in their beautiful masks of soot.
Perish again and again
in a slow delicious swoon.
The moment of death
like a moment of marriage,
the bridegroom, longed-for,
just outside the door. Come
in, they sing. Come in, come in.
And the dead come in,
dragging their next war behind them.

The Wounded Soldier

Now I have a scar down the middle,
like a seam where a pressed tin toy,
a bird or a dog, comes together.
What intimacies, that the doctor
has seen my clockwork. Has had his hands
inside my softness. Who's after me
this time? Napoleon, Bismarck?
Patroclus, the lovely doomed.
I could lie here
in the fragrance of naphtha.

During my worst sickness
I was so lost and hungry
that I went out of myself
into the north hills and over the ice

and only a family of bears
had pity on me. They had taken off
their skins and hung them up
in the hallway, and without them
they looked just like men. Their children
looked just like our children.
For me they boiled meat,

though they ate it raw themselves.
What courtesy. When they were sending me
home they said, *Don't tell the other men
about us; we have children and they deserve
to grow up*. They lifted the dark medal
from over my heart. It's better
to breathe deeply than to be praised.

Why I Don't Do Genealogical Research

If reincarnation is real, if the soul
like a translucent little figurine
passes through the great, pale-blue,
incorporeal, handless Hands
of God on its way to being
something else, then the souls
of the children

whose lives were very thirsty
and very brief, and ended
dreadfully, so dreadfully one hopes
also quickly, these souls must have gone
somewhere, and I may
just possibly be forgiven

for sometimes wishing that,
as they lay there in the sky-colored
Hands, unadorned and clear and fluent
as small lengths of pulled glass,
they might have been lifted,

and tucked, and zipped inside the thick
impossibly soft fur buntings
that are the striped trousers
and silken hoods of my two
cats, Henry and Christopher,

who live with me and have only
to sleep in the sunlight and love
one another, who have fresh
water and carefully measured
food, and regular visits to the kindly
Dr. Schoenberg. One wishes of course

that those children
might inherit the bodies
of statesmen or philanthropists but look:
these sun-sleepers, plush-striped,
I have made such a gentle
life for them, as I would do

even if they did not from time
to time glance at me in a certain
way from their small astonished
orphan's faces, making me think

of the souls of those children,
those dark-coated, pale-kneed
children, who might very well be
my own murdered kinspeople,
plentiful enough as they have been.

II.

War Suite

for my brother

The Family of Skeletons

Wouldn't we have families, too?
Mother, father, three
little ones, all sexless and white
in our home under the hillside
with its many stone doors.
We used to wear flesh, fat, and veins,
we wore our hearts in our breasts like red purses.
We used to wear parkas and aprons
and frocks, burnooses, burqas and trousers,
tallit and shawls. We used to eat blackberries
and bouillabaisse, falafel and cherries,
cheeseburgers with bouquets of hot
yellow fries all shaken with salt.

Now we wear nothing, drink bowlfuls
of air. We live in our cave. Sit
in our green chairs. Roll the dice.
A bright light went off in our life
like the flash of an enormous camera.
Smile, little ones. Say cheese.

The Recruiter

He does not speak. A mask speaks.
His hat and chest are starched.
His heart cramps like a fist,
his tall legs ache, not running.
His mind becomes a net of barbs.
The pimp who lures the beautiful boys
in alleys and in waterbeds: no worse than he.
Unholy shepherd. Fisher of men.

The Parents

Every time we thought to shield
him we wondered out loud, Why
someone else's son and not ours?
So our hands fell to our sides.
We let the devil in the front door,
gave him tea in his own white cup.
The cats in their luscious coats
milled around his legs as if he were human.
Our son's face looked into his face
like a bird charmed by a serpent,
a flower mesmerized by sun.
I know now I should have
let loose the unfriendly dogs.
I should have barred the door
with my own body.

The Widow

Where has he gone,
who moved through me like a river.
Has he broken into a cloud of birds?
A busted fruit, a skein of red pulp?
My mouth is sealed and small
as a sugared rosette.
It no longer opens,
this stopper holding in check
the salt torrent of our bodies.

The Objector

My hands got larger and larger
and there was nothing to do with them.
They grew to plateaus, plains,
each a prairie soft with grasses
and little running, flying things.
Little creeks. And there was no one near.
Language drifted away like steam
from the top of a lake. My hands
were empty and my life so still.
My eyes filled up with time. With sky.
So what if they judged me,
sitting there empty? Sitting there empty
with my hands full of birds.

The Sister

I was asleep a long time, dreaming
of dark sheep with drenched fleeces.
How cool was the grass at my cheek.
And he was only a boy, the littlest goatherd.
Suddenly I awoke. Get away
from my brother, you kings of war.
I am a tuning fork, split-legged, vibrating ions,
a tree, charged and electric,
just struck by lightning, poised
any moment to go up in flame.

Book of Ikons

Ikon for Osip Mandelstam

For you I would rename this kinship of stars
Salt on the Ax-Handle. Over your left shoulder a forest
of conifers burns but is not consumed,
so nothing troubles the wolves beneath their branches
like blue shadows. Your eyes are the dark eyes of a swan;
through the air in formation like a flock of winter geese
the Hellenic ships sweep the wind with their sails,
and to your finger the goldfinch has come
in his yellow cape, the dark asterisks
of his feet. Stouthearted, last seen mad in a transit camp—
black bread, the black rot of wet stumps—
and salt on the ax blade, Osip, for your sake.

Ikon for Rosa Luxemburg

When you first crossed the border to Germany
you came covered up, hidden in a wagon like a tumbrel.
That sour little country, still the hope of your Europe,
where you made an uneasy home, a mouse
in a knife-drawer. Sturdy engine, you, squat and self-
sufficient economy, in your good boots with your limp,
the frilled lip of your oyster-shaped hat, your murderous red language:
they killed you in the Eden Hotel and put you
in a river. I want to believe the last words you said
you said in German. I want to believe you said
Don't Shoot. But hush now—here you are—
not in prison, weeping over a beaten ox,
not beside yourself in August 'fourteen
but in the meadow you loved so much,
up to your waist in the deep grass
and wild flowers, your eyes covered
with a bright visor of light.

Ikon for Angelica Balabanoff

Aging and small, your soft braids cross your crown
like arms on the chest of a white sleeper.
Before you, in your dim eternal student's room,
the table, the spirit-stove, the teapot, and then
your own ikons—Jaurès, Luxemburg, Bebel—as many
as will fit with room still to sit a guest for tea.
You always were poor and neat and energetic
and hopeful. In your right hand, a Ukrainian egg
with its lucid geometry of colors. In your left,
a matryoshka. The outermost doll smiles the secret
smile of the sphinx—nothing like you—
the innermost is blunt as a knucklebone,
a nub with a blurred, inconclusive face
perhaps like your face that terrible year
when at last your nerves failed you,
as the revolution swallowed its own tail.
The party paid for your nurse and how sad it was
for your friends to see the portrait of Big Brother
Togliatti somebody had hung in your room.

Ikon for Käthe Kollwitz

I can feel your crosshatchings on my body:
little wounds. Ink or charcoal, your black is the black
of the childhood room before sleep. Your whole
world divides into light and shadow, even
your skipping, syncopated name: a child
tripping up the museum steps and then the slow
ponderous gait of the mother behind it.
The hands you render broad as oar blades,
eloquent black mittens with intelligent
knuckles and bright nailbeds. You said "Vote!"
You said "Seed Corn Must Not Be Ground!"
And you showed the faces of the mourners
before the body of Liebknecht. Your son
died in a trench, wretched. In your self-portrait
you regard yourself curiously, but without any pity,
cheek in palm. Yet when I look again you have altered,
you have put your face behind your hand,
that dark articulate spade.

Ikon for Karl Kautsky

Idea-architect, the red rainbow
flutters behind you like an academic sash.
The sky itself is robin's egg green and fretted
with cracks. And here you sit in your dark suit
and neat beard, like a good scholar.
Like a good scholar, you were hopeful
but you knew when the truth had to be faced.
Your eyes are formal and sad. One of them
sees revolution. The other sees the day after revolution.
You know you see neither in Russia.
You know that whatever it is you want
for the people, violence unfits them for it.
Your third eye, which no one can see, looks out anxiously
as you wait by the coffee pot for the last two men
of German social democracy to come home
from their walk. You are right to be worried.
They are picking off your friends one
by one. A whole constellation of stars put out,
fondest uncle—singly at first, and then all at once.

Exile Diptych

Brecht in Svendborg

The island floats further from Germany.

And she who had so long inhabited
the carriage and the gait of queens,
peasants, war profiteers, becomes
suddenly and erotically herself:
swimming, her hair unlovely.

But he is abstracted
as an emperor in exile,
salt at his throat.

The white mouse in the lungs
of the little teacher
momentarily stops its gnawing.

The recording angel arrives
in his rumpled suit, plays chess,
departs unadvisedly.

Orion perishes again
and lies down in heaven.

On pale days we can just see
their coats moving among the larches.

Brecht in Hollywood

On the soundstage they've made
Alps green with carpeting.
The resting fräuleins with their smooth
braids and pale temples
have big American teeth.
Their lederhosen are embroidered
with flowers and they wear tap shoes.
But what of blonde Germany, blood-
gloved, sitting with her feet in the ashes?

He goes about in his long coat.
An actress in fox fur takes him
for someone else in the street
and has never heard his name.
She wears a diamond so clear
it makes him thirsty to look at it
and walks a Pyrenees mountain
dog on a gold leash. The dog's
nose is wet and steaming
like a doused coal. And his friend,
the refugee W.B., who died
crossing those mountains, what of him,
who took his life at the Spanish border?

In the street he sees
a white actor in red makeup
and a sombrero (Sancho in his poncho)
and follows him for a while like an old knight.
At the soundstage they bring the actor a donkey
for his scene and Brecht is reminded so cuttingly
of his Svendborg study, its heavy beam bearing
the legend "Truth is concrete" and the little wooden mule

hung with the sign, "I too must understand it."
It seems there must be something true
behind these illusions, but before his eyes,
which have toppled capitols, the walls hold.

Dear Union

"The E.U. is deeply harmful. It is an anti-democratic monster.
I want to prevent it from getting fatter, from continuing to breathe,
from grabbing everything with its paws."

– Marine LePen

Grow fatter, continental monster!
Breathe your dear and snuffling breaths.
Grab everyone, grab everything, and grab
me, too, with your raisin-scented paws,
soft as brötchen, warm as Viennese coffee.
Live long, beast of peace!

Cartoonish face, sniffing the coast,
lapping the salty cliffs, peering under the rushes
to see what is happening in that thatched-roof house,
your muzzle is soft with pollen from the wild
flowers that grow from Oxford walls. Your spine
is made of bridges. Poles and Germans will have a party
on your back. The music makes you shiver!
But with pleasure!

Grow your fur lush and dense. Wolves
and thickset ponies will return to race
your flanks. Wear a raft
of solar panels as your hat!
I want to see you armored
like an armadillo
with embraces,
wearing a saddle of languages,
nosing the crimson lifejackets
in the foam and delighting
the exhausted children,

I want to see you feint
and dance, the arrows of the petty
glancing off your universities
and hookah bars. Grow green

with parks! Gobble dumplings! Crash
the statues to the ground and let new ones
grow from budding trees. Beguile
and charm anyone sour enough
to want to stop you. Unlikely
creature of even unlikelier
benevolence, gambol and live long.
I want touch down, like days of old,
board the beloved Tegel bus
and careen into your goodness.

III.

Der Anfang

A toothed beginning,
like a red enamel comb,
cool in the hand and useful,
but with the shine of ritual danger.
The red comb, the shears,
the dictionary heavy
on its lectern. Sun
on the flagstones. The little dog
is asleep. Come in, this room is for you,
with its great ceiling beams
and fine tools. Even the human
skull is for you. Even the sunlight.
Even the round red hat
that hangs on the wall.
Sit at the desk, make yourself
busy and quiet. This lion
is your brother, who lies
on the floor quiescent,
offering the loaves of his paws,
his tail like a flaxen tassel,
his coat of silk and muscle,
his face, his heavy, eastern face
oblique as a slumbering language.

Der Bär

When you were a child
you were just like a child
with a dark curious face
and a hood and coat
of silken fur. You walked
on two legs, on stout soft feet
and cried for your supper.
You drank milk from a cup
and broke the golden comb
of honey in your paws. Little one,
badge of the beloved city. When
you were a man, you lay by the fire
sad and sick. The maidens
combed your fur. Poor enchanted
thing: how you longed to shrug out
of the hot, heavy skin,
show them your real self:
the pale prince's body,
its lean haunches and elegant
feet, the thousand expressions
of its naked face, the cock
no longer laughable,
the pink tongue, mobile
and strange; no longer mute.

Die Courage

Everything soft or tender,
be banished. Anything that asks
mercy, be exiled. A hard
cheese, that's what you are,
sinewy, and with a voice
like smoke or a spice grater.
Your caustic joy,
tambourine and ankle.
I followed you all
through the woods,
through the bogs
and the shining mud.
You always had
a chicken leg to gnaw,
but you never noticed
how the yellow leaves
pasted over the fallen
after they had coughed
and coughed and coughed.
Your daughter beat
a drum in her silence.
Foolish woman.
Go find your son.

Dunkel

It's true that it's dark. True,
too, that no spine
is happy. Before I heard, yes,
I was laughing. Laughing showed
I hadn't heard. Then—you see
my corrugated forehead. Proof
enough. We eat,
others don't; that's not the right
formula. It's because they don't
eat that we do. A glass of water
is never only itself, but it is
itself, always. Attend. I think
with me around, tyrants may sit
a little bit less lusciously. There is
such a thing as goodness. There is
also such a thing as the flood. We
may go under. Recall us. We did
not do enough, but have pity
for us, nonetheless. To understand
is not exclusively to forgive.

Etwas

A green word, professorial,
like a pediatrician with minty
breath. You're in bed. There is
no longer any region of the dotted
sheet that feels cool to your achy
legs, and the bedside table is cluttered
with glasses and story books, a thermometer
that reads your temperature in celsius
by the movement of its gob of silver
mercury. The doctor is here, with his
bright, moist eyes and dry hands.
His shaved throat is bluish.
He leaves you with sweet chalky
pills, some orange syrup
to drink; you are feeling better
already, relieved and sleepy.
He has always been the formal
doctor so-and-so, but as she closes
the door behind him, your mother says,
gratefully, "Thank you, Etwas,"
some intimate, greenish name, or at least,
as you're falling asleep,
that's what it sounds like.

Die Familie

The father, blue-eyed,
is everywhere at once:
putting the rice on,
puréeing the yellow
squash, tossing the cubed
meat, pink, in the pan, saying,
*It makes a good meal
for the children*, then slicing
his thumb, daubing blood
at sink and mirror in the search
for a band-aid. The mother,
brown-eyed and selkie-haired,
sits slender and sock-footed
at the table keeping me company.
We each have a glass of purple
wine. She wants me to talk
and to show me books. I am
embarrassed to have come
without flowers. She carries
her mind behind her brow
like a beautiful crystal. I am
shy in her pure attention. Then
the children come, and eat
from shallow oval-shaped
dishes, dreaming back
and forth in English
and in German. They have
invited me in, but like a ghost
I can't speak, can't enter.

Genau

A satisfying word,
but absurd, too, friendly
and gregarious, it makes me laugh
the way you might laugh
at some species of mountain
goat clambering up a ridiculous
mountain-side: lizard-eyed,
flop-eared, with convolving
horns and icepick feet, the way
this goat might look back at you
with the blue sky soaring
all around it and the thin wind
ruffling its fur like milkweed,
the way this creature of cloud,
sinew, and gut might say to you
out of its black-lipped, black-
gummed mouth, with its pink
tongue and ungulate teeth,
*Come on! We're almost
there!* How idiotic you'd feel,
yet how happy, scrambling
the rocks in your harness.

Die Hexe

She's here, she is here
the little burning peg.
Marrow and plug, plug
and marrow. You have sought
her out, and knocked the brass
knock, you have followed the steps
that approach her front door:
from her back door, no foot
steps lead. Soft on a mat
of gold needles, acorns
hide their helpless faces.
And here she is now,
her wand a lacquered twig.
Her head's half red,
half white, alight like a pudding.
She eats children, drinks
stones? Her bed is of coals?
She sleeps in an oven?
Is it true? You can ask.
Her ears are full of secrets.

Immer

No city can compete
with this city, capital
of ghastliness, beauty,
and dawn. White sky,
the streetlamps turning
out like diamonds
going dark. A wet kitten
drinks milk on a windowsill.
The drowned girl makes her long way
down the river, under bridges.
Her eyes are looking at
the moon. To her fingers
come the fish, like swallows.
The night's bodies tend
morgueward. A war-hero,
legless, sharpens pencils
readied like a clutch of arrows.
Mothers are ironing. Children
are sleeping in rooms papered
with money, patterns of leader-
faces, wheat-sheaves and stars.
The sun is rising. The street
cleaner comes, as ever.

Jemand

Stout skirt of soil,
the stove formidable.
Stew-maker. Lap-
bearer. Proprietress,
night fortress. A gruffer
gesture. Round blue window,
little dark. Morning porridge.
You don't know who you are but
you're someone.
Red hounds in the afternoon.
Forget about the opera. But
then she's whistling
Queen of the Night.
Water wheel, flying arias.
Forget any black pegasus.
Learn to read again, like
new. You don't know
who you are, you idiot,
but you're someone.

Der Kummer

This is the song she plays
in her white dress and pink
ribbons, the poignant tune
she and the piano sing together.
This is also the word
the old physician, coy
beneath his powdered wig,
ascribes to your condition.
Poor man, swollen-hearted, your soul
throbs in every nerve. How
can you bear to see her intended
lift from the grass the hem of her scarf?
She puts bluebells and violets
in his hair, he's laughing.
He has two pistols, pearly,
neither loaded, and yellow leaves
upon his shoulders. She plays
her little song; it pricks
your sprained heart with every
note. The rain has wrapped its wet
hair round the house; you are so
thirsty. The old physician is asleep,
the piano goes on playing. He's brushing off
those yellow leaves. Might you not now
catch his eye with yours, his mouth with yours,
might your heart not break like an egg,
might not happiness flow out?

Das Lebewohl

Even an umbrella can't comfort
the boar without bristles, the poor
skinned rabbit, tender. Saddest
things: soup pots, wire snares,
train schedules, stop watches,
telephones. Keep on bandaging
my forearm, says Patroclus,
pulling away with no pants on.
Don't let the story move one inch
forward. You're always getting
left behind in Moscow or disappearing
into the effervescent Zeus-beard
of a waterfall. And there is always
someone watching dumbly, suffering,
doctor's bag waiting at the door.
Breasts are bared and beaten, handkerchiefs
get snuffy. If it were a thousand years
ago, we wouldn't cry. That's not
true. We'd be crying all the time.

Der Mittelstand

Dinner at a table whose cloth
is thick and stiff as writing paper.
The plates are blank clock-faces,
the forks bristle and proliferate.
The coffee urn, silver, burbles
on the sideboard like a magistrate
with indigestion. Sister's bows
are black moths posing captive
on her head, mother has plucked
the teeth of whales to make
a second set of ribs. Father's
mustaches depend. Brother's
feet don't reach the floor, but
his shoes make sparks, colliding.
The carpet pattern repeats itself
to itself. The roast says
nothing. No one speaks of cousin
Manfred, who hates everything. Inside
their breasts their golden hearts roar
and pace, like lions kept in birdcages.

Niemand

Who was he? Nobody.
With a face like the face of the moon,
changeable. The impressions
of his features only light
suggestions. Hypodermic
in one hand, pencil in the other.
As a young man he learned
medicine, but the dark bag
got lost in a field somewhere,
overturned and ransacked, inhabited
by the softest species of mice.
They live in the lining. But
what mouths opened for him?
What stages, where actors sit
disconsolate, waiting for his scenes?
He only thinks of the ways he cannot
help, never of the ways he helps.
The staircase has a long banister,
an elegant wife gets her own
ideas. We can never return
to the days of blue horses,
he thinks. Just a face like a moon,
looking up from the riverbottom.

Ohne

I wrote this word on your tree,
leaving the island in a hurry.
I hope you will know what it means
and how to find me. We agreed
about this once, but it was long ago.
I think you will remember, though.
When the stars are pointing north,
when the arrow's robed in ice,
when the seals sleep on the slick
black living lace that coats the rocks—
then the boat will build its wings,
then the lyre makes a path,
wear your warmest skirts and come
over the hill along the coast.
The knife was hard to hold,
the tree slipped left. But you will see
the word I carved and know,
I know, to come at once,
dearest sister, dearest brother,
across the sea and over,
over the nighttime sea.

Die Pferde

These creatures with breathing blue
necks. Arch and bristle. Forelock and star.
They come rushing over the horizon
like clouds, and our hearts wilt
to see them. For there is no saddle
so splendid it could coax them to hold
us. They open their mouths for no
bit. Oh god, the grace of blue
horses. They are always passing
away into the endless. They are gone,
taking the blue river stones of their shoulders,
the rain points of their legs, their windy
tails and their manes stiff as the ruff
of a war helmet. Yet these are creatures
who have never suffered on the battlefield.
No, they know nothing of that. So
they have gone. But here come their red
cousins, blazing and gorgeous, bucking
over the sky. They too are innocent
and their ears are never the soft ears
of the defeated one who drops his lips
to the ruined earth, to the ruined shoulder
of the painter who will not get up again.

Der Quellbach

The first thing is never to be precious
about the puppets. Let them
be. They might sit slumped on a shelf,
they might hang over the back of a chair.
Do not be seduced by any power you imagine
is theirs without you. Beware of feeding
them soup, beware of speaking to them
if you have belted them into the backseat
of the car. No, to have real respect
for these figures, you must know when the soul
in them is sleeping. You must know
what it means when you shake your whole arm
and they dance. Now you are in relation
to one another. Now the blue light wakes
in the wooden face. Now when you speak
he will listen, he will turn the poor shell
of his ear, the soft flannel of his breast, he
will turn them to you so soulfully, the way
you would, if god ever spoke to you
in the little indigo theater of the world.

Reden

This is what I cannot do
without blushing. Words
won't come. Not with your
hands clasped just so. So:
You wore a big coat. So,
again, you were young.
In the moonlight, by a pond,
in white, a woman. These
books read in a fever,
out loud, in a foreign place.
The lamp, the pillow, the trace;
the gold spot on the old
quilt where I set my plum.
Her throat doesn't interest you;
don't play dumb. It's the eyebrow,
the individual quirk of the thumb.
Storm-mind, illuminate me.
Detective, move my tongue.

Die Seele

Round-headed, round-eyed,
curious, astonished,
like an owl or a sea lion,
but white as moonlight:
a lynx with feathered feet,
bounding. Hello, you silence.
Hello, you secret joy. Take flight
into the blackest forest
where the wild boar
still roots with a coral-pink
snout. Let him find you
his own prize, bloom of earth,
a truffle: that ruffled treat,
like an ugly rose in the hand,
the friendly earth's delicious
gift. I don't care what they say,
how many drawings they do
of you in a dead baby's
nightgown: I know you love
the things of this world,
and will miss them, when you go.

Der Tod

He is wearing
his white armor.
His helmet smiles,
but there is nothing
light-hearted about him.
He may speak with you
respectfully, he may
beat you so beautifully
at the chessboard it breaks
your heart. Don't believe
his poetry. Don't apprehend
his song. You don't
want to know how tender
he is with the children,
how they know how to trust
him. You don't want to look
at his terrible horse,
or the way he makes love,
impossibly sweetly, or see
how he carries away
the last kisses of your wife
like a posy of white flowers.

Ungefähr

The name of a princess:
one with yellow braids
and a serious mouth,
rose-like, but with two
lines around it, one on each
side, as if needle-etched;
with a fine collarbone
and a blue dress that falls
straight down, severely,
to the toes of her pointed shoes,
who rides out wearing her brother's armor
when knights have gone astray
and lie with their hair in the river
in thrall to some grand idea.
A virgin on a horse
in winter, blurred flakes,
the warrior fallen in her arms
so he rides lying forward
on her horse's wet neck.
Maybe she feels something,
a stirring in her solemn heart.
She is a woman who knows the meaning
of that terrible word, approximately.

Verliebt

Oracular valentine, with the drunk
little black milk snakes curled up
on your forehead. Their tongues
lapped the saucer and they fell
fast asleep. Your heart a black
heart, buttoned on with a mitten.
Under the tree, at attention,
wounded, stoic, poetic, cynical.
Your uncle unfolded his gold
wings; it was he who made the owl's
call, clock-top. You walked backwards,
made a misstep. Restored
a girl. Were condemned. Were
adored. Were wounded, under
your dark curls. The cut
a pink whorl. Little pawn. Prawn.
At dawn, bleary, too beautiful.
You, you who had never shaved,
you who had always worn boots.

Das Wörterbuch

He built himself a house of books.
They took it apart. He wrote new
books. No one would print them.
He sent his library across the ocean.
Then it was safe, but he wasn't. The flat
was too costly. He got an irritating
roommate. She was always weeping.
Life was so hard. Well, so it was.
He climbed inside the horn
of a phonograph. It was deafening,
and three times a day the leader's voice
washed over him, like acid. They
rooted him out with a pair of tweezers.
He was getting smaller every day
and, dangling, he glimmered like a lost earring.
They marched him to a castle. His lungs
sponged up the damp. He tried one
more time to escape. He drank
from a green pond, he ate a tomato,
he dragged along a footpath. Even
his pocket watch was too heavy.
When the borders closed against him,
he tried to slip through, but the space
between spines was too narrow.
He winked out typographically, kerned.

Die Xber

A bad man said that potatoes rest in cellars
just as much as poem books. In cellars
and in knapsacks; both, cracked open,
could nourish armies. Comfort
and warmth, fork and breath. Imagine it
for a moment, the lights in the windows. But snow
doesn't land like powdered sugar
in a wound. Stars that might have opened
up and sung a carol roll like glass eyes
frosty in the bottom of a drawer. That's
the sky, what we did to it. And we shot
the boys we should have loved. We made thunder
hide her comely head in shame, we outdid
thunder. Trees leapt in horror, their roots
slipping from the earth like tubes
out of an arm. The whole world needs
a surgeon. This bluest month goes sluicing
down the drain. A potato for my mouth
and for my ear a poem. I start
my march in Kiel and end in Rome.

Das Yperit

Gentle it into the smell of mustard
greens cooking, to garlic
minced on a board and tossed
into the sizzling fat. Mother is here
to crack eggs into the pan and boil
the lice from your shirt. Father is here,
half-blind now, but still with the good
dirt on his hands, holding a bouquet
of white radishes. Sister, too, jubilant
at your return but hardened somehow,
like a sapling rising within its first bark.
Now look, though. Your books, all your
picture books are here. Here is a knight,
here is a black sow, rotund and kindly. All
these stories, before you could read them.
On the windowsill, the little family
you carved from wood, the stones
you collected when your hands were small
and you washed them every night
before supper. The birch bark you peeled
for writing messages. A spool of red thread
that once spoke to you so ardently. You thought
you could go back, didn't you, and look,
just look, you can. You have. Now forward.

Zusammen

Death, don't talk to me
all the time, just sometimes.
And god won't talk to me
all the time, but sometimes.
Yet you will talk to me
all the time, with your words
and with your silences. So call
the red dogs. Call the bear
in his deep overcoat, wake
him from sleep. Wake the king
curled inside the fur, and wake
the horses, all the horses. Fetch
the lion. Call the birds. If there's bread,
we shall have it. And milk,
and a little chair to sit in. I want a star
glazed and fat as a cake, I want a house
like a nightlight, a road
that leads to the wood's green heart.
Let that which follows us,
intimate and mysterious,
go ahead. Let that which falls away
wave goodbye like a tree.
Call everyone. Call everything loved.
Take my hand. Let's go.

A Note About the Author

Photo courtesy of Adrianne Mathiowetz, © 2019

Katherine Hollander is a poet and historian. Born in Boston, she was educated at Marlboro College and Boston University, where she earned an M.A. in poetry and a Ph.D. in history. Her poems, criticism, and scholarly work have appeared in *Literary Imagination, Slate, Hunger Mountain, Tupelo Quarterly, The Brecht Yearbook, New German Critique*, and elsewhere. She has taught European history at Simmons College, the University of Hartford, and Colby College, creative writing at Boston University, and serves as a Reader for *Sugar House Review*. Alongside writing poems, she is at work on a historical monograph about a community of German-speaking intellectuals in exile, and translating the childhood memoirs of Margarete Steffin.

A Note About the Anthony Hecht Poetry Prize

The Anthony Hecht Poetry Prize was inaugurated in 2005 and is awarded on an annual basis to the best first or second collection of poems submitted.

FIRST ANNUAL HECHT PRIZE
Judge: J. D. McClatchy
Winner: Morrie Creech, *Field Knowledge*

SECOND ANNUAL HECHT PRIZE
Judge: Mary Jo Salter
Winner: Erica Dawson, *Big-Eyed Afraid*

THIRD ANNUAL HECHT PRIZE
Judge: Richard Wilbur
Winner: Rose Kelleher, *Bundle o' Tinder*

FOURTH ANNUAL HECHT PRIZE
Judge: Alan Shapiro
Winner: Carrie Jerrell, *After the Revival*

FIFTH ANNUAL HECHT PRIZE
Judge: Rosanna Warren
Winner: Matthew Ladd, *The Book of Emblems*

SIXTH ANNUAL HECHT PRIZE
Judge: James Fenton
Winner: Mark Kraushaar, *The Uncertainty Principle*

SEVENTH ANNUAL HECHT PRIZE
Judge: Mark Strand
Winner: Chris Andrews, *Lime Green Chair*

EIGHTH ANNUAL HECHT PRIZE
Judge: Charles Simic
Winner: Shelley Puhak, *Guinevere in Baltimore*

A Note About the Anthony Hecht Poetry Prize

NINTH ANNUAL HECHT PRIZE
Judge: Heather McHugh
Winner: Geoffrey Brock, *Voices Bright Flags*

TENTH ANNUAL HECHT PRIZE
Judge: Anthony Thwaite
Winner: Jaimee Hills, *How to Avoid Speaking*

ELEVENTH ANNUAL HECHT PRIZE
Judge: Eavan Boland
Winner: Austin Allen, *Pleasures of the Game*

TWELFTH ANNUAL HECHT PRIZE
Judge: Gjertrud Schnackenberg
Winner: Mike White, *Addendum to a Miracle*

THIRTEENTH ANNUAL HECHT PRIZE
Judge: Andrew Motion
Winner: Christopher Cessac, *The Youngest Ocean*

FOURTEENTH ANNUAL HECHT PRIZE
Judge: Charles Wright
Winner: Katherine Hollander, *My German Dictionary*

Other Books from Waywiser